Experimenting with Light and Illusions

Alan Ward

Illustrated by Zena Flax

CHELSEA JUNIORS
A division of Chelsea House Publishers
New York · Philadelphia

Contents

3 5 7 9 8 6 4

ISBN 0-7910-1514-9

Preface

You are about to discover – through play – just how magical science can seem, when you start to look closely and thoughtfully at the wonderful tricks that light can play on your eyes and mind. You will not forget the beauty and fascination of the simple experiments suggested in this book. The thrills you have from doing them will awaken your interest in the grander ideas now being explored by scientists in every country. No person in future will be fully educated without an understanding of some of the key ideas of science. This book will help you to become a scientifically educated person.

Most of the materials that you need are ordinary and inexpensive, sometimes costing nothing – and they will usually be found somewhere in your home. Mirror tiles are better for the experiments about reflections than framed mirrors. Before starting any of the projects, read the text carefully and make a list of what materials you need.

All kinds of practical work involve some risk of accidents, so take care. Common sense and working in a calm frame of mind are most conducive to safety. Remember that scientists work methodically, with definite ideas about what observations and tests they are doing. Experiments are safe if things like matches, candles and glass bowls are handled sensibly. Never "fool about" with science. Have fun and enjoy yourself, while remembering that you are responsible for your actions. Some of the activities in this book are about the sun. You must never look directly at the sun.

How to make rainbows

Sunlight is white light. Its light is so strong that you must never look straight at the sun, because it can damage your eyes and make you blind.

But notice how the whiteness of sunlight brings out the colors in all things: flowers, old walls, carpets and wall-paper.

If a ray of sunlight is allowed to enter and come out from clear wedge-shapes called prisms, that are made from glass, plastic or water, the light is split into several different rays. You see these as lovely colors: red, orange, yellow, green, blue, indigo and violet – called the colors of the sun's spectrum (the solar spectrum).

A water-prism

Fill a plastic box or deep tray with water. Put it down on the floor, or on a table, in front of a window through which bright sunlight is coming. Do this when the sun is fairly low down in the sky.

Slant a mirror in the water, pointing it towards the sun. A pebble in the water will stop the mirror from slipping. **Do not look at the sun** while you are setting the mirror. Look at the wall or ceiling around the window.

After a little time spent in getting the water and mirror in just the right positions, you will see a beautiful band of pure spectral colors where the reflected sunlight strikes.

Tape (or hold) a piece of white paper where the colors appear, to make a screen. The colors are clearest and purest while the water is kept still.

If you disturb the water by wagging your finger in it, the colors blur and mix – to make white (the mixed light they came from in the first place).

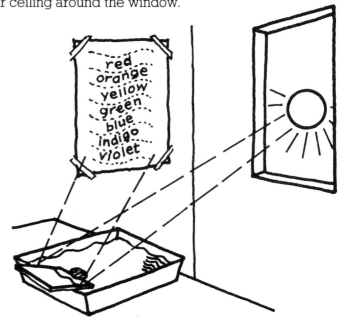

Circular rainbow

In the morning or evening, when the bright sun is low in the sky, stand with your back to the sun and squirt a fine spray of water from a hose-pipe pointed at a dark background of trees or walls. Look into the spray to see a beautiful rainbow. It will appear small and circular. Rainbows look circular from airplanes.

The water drops act both as prisms and as mirrors to make the rainbow you see. Real rainbows happen like this. You do not normally see circular rainbows from ground level because they are too wide and appear too low for you to see the full circle.

Look for rainbows in sprays of water from waterfalls.

Looking for rainbows

1 Obtain a clear, plastic ballpoint-pen case – the kind that has six narrow, flat sides. In bright sunlight, hold the casing near a sheet of white paper. Hold and twist the casing, until a pale spectrum appears on the paper. The shaped plastic acts like a prism.

2 Borrow a piece of finely cut "crystal" glass, such as the stopper from a wine decanter. Hold and twist this object in bright sunlight, near a white wall. The shaped glass acts like a mass of prisms. You should be able to get some attractive spectra projected on to the wall.

3 Stand a glass of water just inside a window, where sunlight is streaming through. Put a big sheet of white paper on the floor, just below the glass. Move about the glass until rainbow colors appear on the paper. White light passing through the curved wedge-shape of water at the edge of the surface is split to form a spectrum.

Kaleidoscopes

Use sticky tape to make a hinge between two mirrors or mirror tiles. Stand up the mirror tiles like this.

Put a few flowers and leaves between the mirrors. Observe the beautiful patterns formed by the reflections. Try other objects: your hand, colored wool, a handkerchief, beads ...

What happens to the pattern when you change the angle between the mirrors? (Perhaps the most pleasing patterns are made with the mirrors at 60°.) You could copy and color the patterns, or photograph them.

Fix together three mirror tiles, using rubber bands. Their reflecting surfaces should be inside the triangle. (All the angles will be 60°.)

You could put flowers and insects inside, or a pet mouse (be gentle). Imagine being inside with your friends. To give you some idea, put small dolls or toy soldiers inside and observe their reflections inside this "Magic Room".

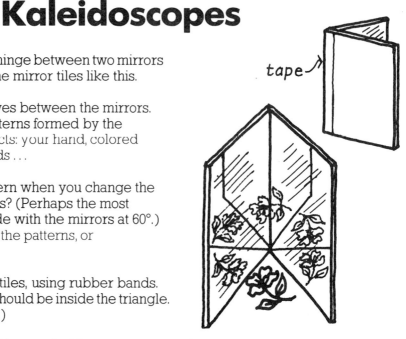

How a kaleidoscope works

The size of a reflection and the distance it appears to be "inside" a flat mirror are the same as the actual size and distance of the object from the mirror. But left and right are reversed.

Circle number 1 represents the object. A and B represent two mirrors hinged together at an angle of 60°.

Mirror A reflects the object at 2a, and the mirror B at C. Mirror B reflects the object at 2b, and the mirror A at D. Reflected mirror C reflects 2a at 3a, and mirror A at E. Reflected mirror D reflects 2b at 3b, and mirror B at F. The last reflection (4) is formed from overlapping reflections of 3a and 3b in reflected mirrors E and F. Alternate images are reversed sideways (from left to right).

The six-part pattern with this arrangement of mirrors is made up of one object (1) and five reflections (2a, 2b, 3a, 3b, 4). Another name for a "reflection" is an "image". The pattern consists of one object and five images.

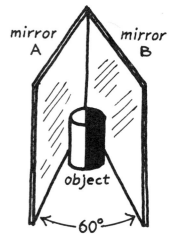

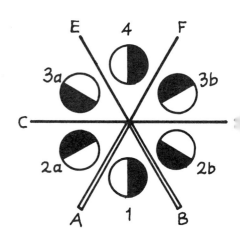

The sum of the images in a kaleidoscope — by arithmetic

Count the images in hinged mirrors open at 90°, 60°, 45° and (perhaps) 30°. Use a protractor to help you with the angles.

Each part of the pattern is inside an angle.
The parts form a circle.
There are 360° in a circle.

A perfect pattern is formed when 360 divided by the angle of the mirrors gives a whole-number answer.

Let the angle between the mirrors be x°.
Then the number of images can be calculated by arithmetic.
You divide 360 by x and subtract 1 from the answer. (This should work for the images you counted.)
A mathematician writes it like this: $n = (\frac{360}{x}) - 1$.

angle of mirrors	number of images
90°	
60°	5
45°	
30°	

Lively patterns

Hinge together two mirrors. (Lightweight plastic mirrors are best.) Fix their bottom ends in two slots that are first cut in corks that can then be stuck to a board. The mirrors should be at 60°, and their lower edges should be about 0.2 in above the level of the board.

Cut out a cardboard circle and pin its center just under the taped hinge of the mirrors. It must be possible to turn this circle on its pin, under the mirrors.

Draw colored scribbles, or funny faces, or little animals on the circle. Then make it turn while you look at the reflections in the mirrors. The effects are amazing.

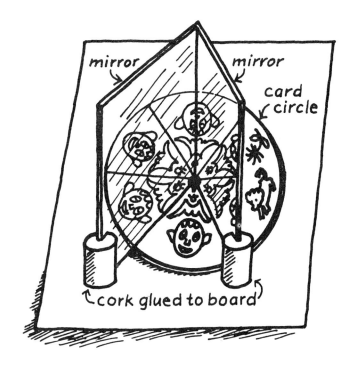

mirror mirror card circle cork glued to board

Pepper's ghost

A sheet of glass (or perspex plastic) can act like a mirror as well as like a window. Stand it up straight on a tray, by pressing one corner into Plasticine. **Take care not to cut yourself.** Wait until it is getting dark, or draw the curtains. You also need two fat candles, exactly the same. Light one candle (A) and stand it up about 6 in in front of the glass. **Do not have an accident with the fire**.

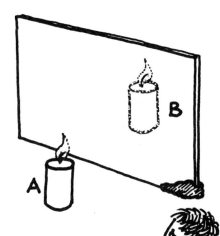

You see a reflection of the candle in the glass. Then take the second candle (B) and carefully move it *behind* the glass, until it fits exactly into the reflection of A. It looks as if candle B gets lit – by magic . . .

Or, you could look at the reflection of A while you move a hand behind the glass – to put your fingers into the *reflection* of the candle flame. If you put a bowl of goldfish there, instead of a hand, or candle B, it looks as if the candle is burning underwater.

The experience with the second candle proves that an object and its image in a plane (flat) mirror are the same size. And, by taking measurements, you can show that distances of object and image to the "mirror" are equal too.

How to haunt a theatre

Now you can understand an optical illusion invented over a century ago and made famous by the showman John Henry Pepper. In a small theatre a special stage was built. Under the stage, out of sight of the audience, an actor, dressed like a horrifying ghost and well-lit by a spotlight, was reflected by a large ordinary mirror set at an angle. Above this mirror was an enormous sheet of plate glass, reaching right across the stage. The actor's reflection in the mirror was itself reflected out into the eyes of the audience by the see-through glass. (The people did not know the glass was there.) The "ghost" appeared to be amongst the real actors on the stage.

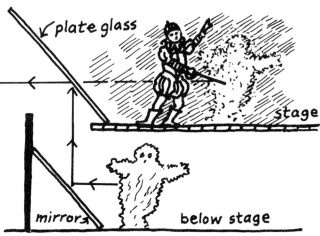

If this is hard to understand, look out into a dark garden through the window of a well-lit room. You will "see" your own ghost "out there" amongst the midnight flowers.

"Death" in Paris

"The Tavern of the Dead" was a sensational variation of Pepper's Ghost, performed in a dimly-lit Paris night-club.

Non-reflecting black screens and backgrounds hid a brilliant white model of a skeleton that could be illuminated by spotlights.

A lady or gentleman volunteer from the audience was wrapped in a white shroud and stood inside a coffin that was well-lit by concealed lights. The audience could see this happening very clearly.

Then, while the attention of the audience was distracted, a huge sheet of plate glass was silently pushed out, at an angle, from behind the stage.

As spooky music was played, the lights shining on the coffin were slowly dimmed, at the same time as the lights pointed at the skeleton were lit and slowly brightened.

Gradually the person inside the coffin became invisible to the audience, and seemed to dissolve – in the minds of the audience – into the deathly *reflection* of the skeleton.

These procedures were reversed to make the person in the coffin "come alive" again.

Mirror magic

Use Plasticine to fix a comb, with its teeth pointing upwards, just in front of a board or box-lid. Aim the comb at the sun – but **do not look at the sun.** Let white light shine through the teeth, to form parallel (side-by-side) rays, making white lines. Notice how light usually travels in straight lines. That is why light casts shadows, and why you cannot normally see around corners.

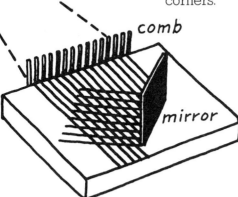

Hold a plane mirror, with its edge touching the board, in the path of the rays. Observe how the mirror reflects them. *Angles formed with the mirror before and after reflection are always equal.* This helps to explain how you see yourself in a plane mirror.

Rays from points A and B travel to the mirror, where they are reflected back to your eyes. You do not sense that the rays are bouncing off the mirror. Your brain believes that they are coming from points A1 and B1 (that seem to be behind or "inside" the mirror).

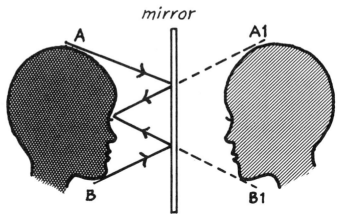

To make mirror-writing

Put carbon paper, carbon side up, on a magazine. Use an inkless ballpen to write a message on paper which you have put over the carbon. Read the writing by looking at its image in a mirror.

How tall does a mirror have to be to reflect your full height?

Find a picture of a person standing up. Paste it on cardboard. Cut out the figure and bore a peephole between its eyes. By looking through this hole – from the back of the card – to observe the image of the figure in an upright wall mirror, you can imagine that you *are* the little figure looking at its own reflection.

Hold still, while you mark felt-pen lines on the mirror, to record where you see the top and bottom of the image. The distance between the lines will be half the height of the cut-out (roughly).

This experience proves that you can see your entire standing self reflected in a mirror which is only half your height.

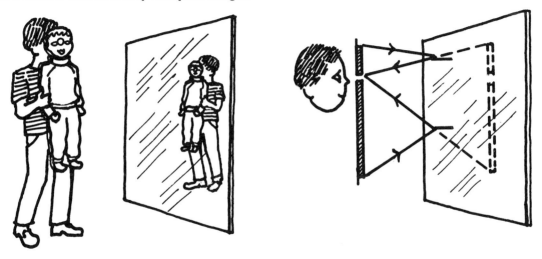

A question that will drive you crazy ...

People ask: How can a mirror reverse left and right without reversing top and bottom?

Imagine your face as a rubber mask. A mirror image is like the mask turned inside-out. What was the back of the mask is now the front. It would be more correct to say that a mirror reverses front and back.

But we always judge left and right from the front, so when, by mirror magic, "back" has to be called "front", our *judgement* of left and right is reversed. Top and bottom are not affected if we think about the mirror image in this way.

Calling the back of a flat cut-out letter **R** its front makes it read like **Я** This explains mirror-writing.

More mirror magic

Reflecting a reflection

The picture shows a clock reflected in a special mirror made by joining two plane mirrors with tape and standing them up at 90° to each other. In such a mirror there is double reflection (left and right are reversed, then reversed again to be as they were before) – and so the image looks the same as the object.

Can you use this "mirror" to read your mirror-writing? Look into it and wink an eye. What you see makes you feel weird.

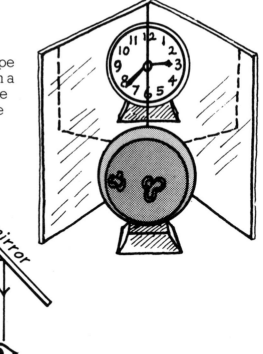

Mystery words

Print "MAGIC MAN", "CODE BOOK" and "CHOICE QUALITY" on separate papers. Hold a mirror upright, along the top edge of each printed paper, and observe the reflections of the words. The first look upside-down, the second look the right way up, but the third look half inverted and half upright, when their images are viewed in the mirror.

Can you explain the mystery?

Then print the words on a paper, like this:

Turn the words upside-down (by turning the paper top to bottom). Then look at the words through the *back* of the paper, while holding the paper up to the light. What do you see?

Now explain that!

A periscope

A periscope can be used to see over the heads of people in a crowd. Make a periscope by fixing two small, lightweight mirrors on to a ruler, using Plasticine, like this. (The mirrors must be slanted at angles of 45° to the ruler.)

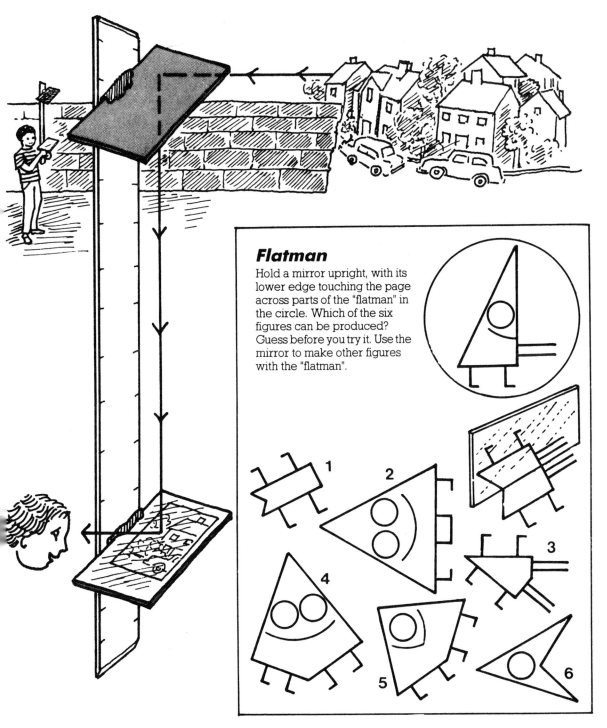

Flatman

Hold a mirror upright, with its lower edge touching the page across parts of the "flatman" in the circle. Which of the six figures can be produced? Guess before you try it. Use the mirror to make other figures with the "flatman".

Bent light

Put a penny in the middle of a big mixing bowl. It might be wise to fix it there with Plasticine. Look along a line of sight, over the edge of the bowl. *Keep still* while somebody fills the bowl with water. (You could fix your eye position by peeping through a hole in a card, bent to stand upright.) As the bowl fills, the penny appears to swim into sight.

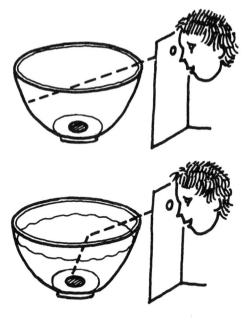

But the penny and your sight line are fixed. What has changed? Light reflected by the penny – which you were unable to see before – now comes into your line of sight. To do this, the light must bend. It bends towards your line of sight when it leaves the water. Underwater, as in air, light usually travels in straight lines.

Think about the penny trick. When you observe the penny while it is underwater, it appears to be higher than where you know it must be. Also, the depth of the water seems less. Water in a swimming pool is always deeper than it looks – so take care.

---

image appears here,
making the stick look bent

real stick

Stick tricks

The explanation of the penny trick will help you to understand how a stick that is partly dipped in water appears to be bent.

Try these light tricks with a stick and glass jar filled with water. The curved glass shapes the water into a magnifying lens. Lenses work by bending light.

More evidence that light can bend

You need a rectangular plastic lunchbox, or something similar, that is transparent. Fill the box with water. Stand it on a sheet of paper. Rest a peashooter (minus its mouthpiece) behind the box, so that it touches at an angle of about 50°.

Look through a second peashooter tube from the opposite side of the box – through the water – at the first tube. Arrange the tube along which you are sighting so that you can see light coming to you from the far end of tube one. Let both tubes rest on the paper.

Stand back and look down on the tubes through which the light "beam" came to your eye. *The tubes are not in line.* The light coming through the first tube must have bent when it entered the water and (assuming it travelled straight through the water) it must have bent again when it passed from the water into the second tube.

When light bends like this it is said to be refracted.

To spear a fish you must aim closer to yourself than where the fish appears.

A fisherman's secret

Refraction is the secret of yet another mystery. Draw two equal fishes touching a line ruled on a paper. Rest the box of water over one of the fishes. Notice that the "underwater" fish looks higher up and a little further back than where you know it must be. (The second fish acts as a control, to help you make the comparison.)

Refraction Circus

Refractory Arrow

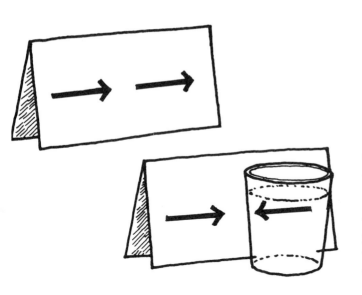

Draw two right-pointing arrows, about 4 in apart, on a card that you can stand up. Some distance in front of one of the arrows (you will have to experiment) stand an empty glass.

Keep watching the arrow behind the glass, as you pour in water to fill the glass. The arrow behind the glass (now a water-lens) changes direction.

Another arrow trick

Cut an arrow-shaped hole, about 2 in long, in a piece of black paper. Let sunlight shine through the hole, to project an arrow shape on the floor.

Hold a magnifying-glass between the paper and the floor. Be patient, and you will get the arrow on the floor to point the opposite way.

Headless soldier

Stand a toy soldier up to its neck in water, inside a plastic box or an aquarium. To "behead" the soldier, look through the side of the container, but "at an angle".

You see light coming directly to you from the head, but light coming out from underwater is refracted and seems to be coming from an unlikely place.

Puzzles with water-lenses

Get a smooth, straight-sided (cylinder-shaped) glass jar, measuring about 2 in across. Nearly fill it with water. Dip in your thumb and examine it through the side of the jar. The glass shapes the water into a kind of lens. Does your thumb look longer, shorter, fatter, thinner?

Now *imagine* pushing a ping-pong ball under the water. Try to draw what it will look like. (Perhaps you think it will be egg-shaped, but will the "egg" appear to be upright, or lying on its side)?

Check your guess by doing a test.

Pour away the water and stand the empty jar in the middle of the plastic box containing water (the box you used in the headless soldier trick). Hold a ruler upright inside the jar. Look at it through the water. Notice how its shape is changed by refraction of light.

Draw your guess of how the ping-pong ball will look when you put it in the jar to replace the ruler. Then do another test. Are you right this time?

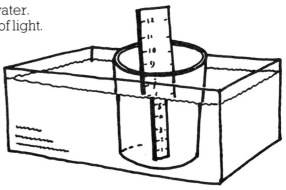

Inside reflections

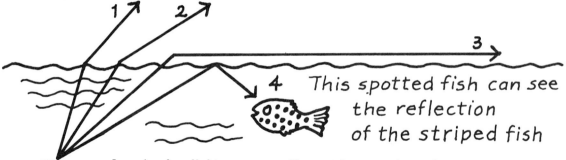

4 *This spotted fish can see the reflection of the striped fish*

Imagine four light rays spreading out from a point underwater and travelling along decreasingly sloping lines to the surface.

Rays 1 and 2 get out into the air, but they are bent down towards the water by refraction. Ray 3 is refracted so much that it actually travels out along the surface. Ray 4 is unable to get out of the water, so what happens to it?

For ray 4 the surface acts like an ordinary mirror.

Reflections inside water

Fill a glass with water. Stand it near the edge of the table. Look up over the table, to see the water's surface from below. If you waggle your fingers on the far side of the glass, you see them reflected in the mirror-like surface.

Copy the funny face on a piece of paper and hold it on the other side of the glass. Look at the reflection of your picture under the water.

"Baldy" grows some hair, but loses his beard . . .

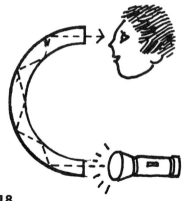

Reflections inside glass

Hold a glass basin sideways with its rim towards you. Shine a flashlight against the lower rim. Some light travels inside the wall of the basin, bouncing to and fro and making a U-bend, and out through the upper rim, back to your eyes.

This experiment is more spectacular in a darkened room.

Understanding a mirage

Light will not travel in straight lines through a transparent substance (water, glass, plastic, air, etc) if there is any variation in the optical density or "thickness" of the substance.

Warm air is thinner (less dense) than cold air, and so light is refracted when it passes from one into the other. You can observe this happening just above the roof of a car on a hot sunny day.

The hot roof heats the air just above it. If you look through the layer of hot rising air, you will notice that the light coming from cooler air, through the moving hot air, gets bent. You see this happening when the background seems to be shimmering.

A desert mirage

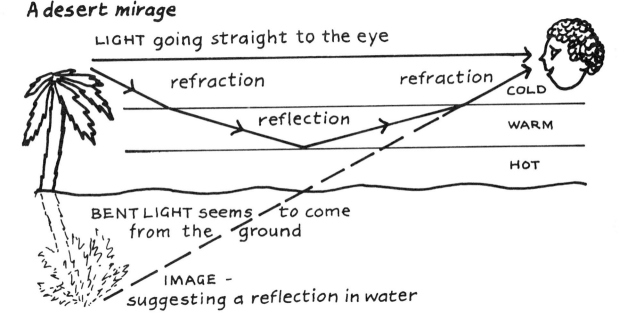

A traveller in a hot desert may see a mirage. Distant rocks or bushes seem to be reflected by the ground, giving the impression that a pool of water is present.

A mirage can be explained by refraction *and* reflection inside the air. Near the ground the air is hot, but higher up the air is cooler.

A mirage on the road

On a hot summer's day, look for a mirage in the distance on a hot road. It will look as if the sky is being reflected by the ground. But you will not be fooled into seeing a pool of water there, will you?

Shadow play

When light strikes anything, some bounces off, some is absorbed ("soaked in") and some may be transmitted ("allowed to pass through").

Sunlight absorbed by furniture, curtains and book-covers fades their colors. Light transmitted by windows makes it possible for us to see through solid brick walls!

When some light is reflected, some absorbed and some transmitted, a shadow is formed; even a candle flame or a soap bubble casts a shadow. But the darkest shadow is produced when no light gets through a body – such as you. Have you ever tried making shadows shaped like butterflies and rabbits, using only your hands?

A century ago, travellers on the Brocken mountain in Germany were frightened by the appearance of what seemed like giant figures looming in the dawn mists. They were scared by a misjudgement of the size of their own shadows, projected on the mists by the rising sun.

Shadows can frighten because they are not always quite like the ordinary, non-frightening objects that make them.

Experiment with a pencil fixed to a long pin, and a bright flashlight, to see the different-shaped shadows possible with this simple object. Can you make the shadow circular or much bigger than the actual size of the pencil?

Also observe shadows out of doors. Can you separate yourself from your shadow? (Try jumping.)

A similar effect to shadows is produced when you see the dark silhouettes of objects, such as trees, against a lighter background. These shapes can be scary too.

Shadow stick to sun-dial

At noon the sun is due South and is at its highest position in the sky. The shadow of an upright stick on level ground will point to North.

On a summer day, mark the end of the stick's shadow with a different pebble every half an hour between 9 and 4 o'clock. Notice how the shadow shortens at first, then lengthens again – as it swings from West to East, and points to North when it is shortest at noon.

You can use the shadow stick and pebbles the next day as a sun-dial, to tell the time.

(By the way, in the Southern Hemisphere of the world, the sun is due North at noon and throws a shadow due South.)

Remember that the stick must be vertical (use a weight dangling from a string to help you) and that the ground must be level (use a builder's level).

You could make the sun-dial on a sheet of paper fixed on a table. The gnomon (the part that produces the shadow) can be anything from a toy soldier to a tall boot. . . . Mark the shadow positions with a pencil.

Something else to do

Here is a puzzle that can be solved by an experiment. How can you use a shadow stick to calculate the height of a tree?

You also need your weight tied to a string (plumbline) and a tape-measure.

Another magic room

In ancient Egypt a poor farmer was put into prison for upsetting the king. His cell was a small, box-like room with a hole in the wall, to let in air. The walls were coated with white plaster. After some time in this unpleasant place, the farmer thought that he must be going crazy, He could see faint-colored pictures of yellow desert, green trees and blue sky. The clouds were moving. But everything was happening upside-down.

Being an intelligent man (perhaps that is why he annoyed the king), he understood the pale and dark pictures. They were produced by light passing through the hole and spreading out to hit the opposite part of the cell.

The prisoner offered to build a "Magic Room" to amuse the king – and, for this, he was given his freedom and enough money to live a more comfortable life.

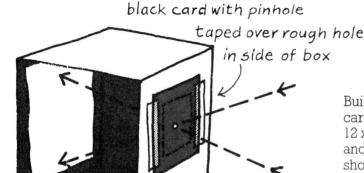

black card with pinhole taped over rough hole in side of box

Build a magic room from a cardboard box measuring about 12 x 9 x 9 in. Paint it black inside and plug any holes. The picture shows where you must paste a white paper screen. Cut a rough hole (1 in square) in the side opposite the screen. Prick a neat tiny pinhole in a piece of black cardboard and tape this card over the rough hole – with the pinhole in the middle. Light will enter the box through the hole. through the hole.

MY TURN NEXT!

You also need a very dark cloth. Cover yourself with the cloth. Hold the box, with its open side towards you, and drape the cloth around and under the box – forming a sort of room, with you inside and where light can enter only through the hole. Point the hole at some brilliant scenery and be amazed by the dim, but colored and moving, upside-down pictures on the screen. Get somebody to help with the cloth.

The secret of the magic room

Make a pinhole in the middle of a thin black card. Bend the card to make it stand up.

Stand a lighted candle in a dish of sand and put the dish 4 in or so to one side of the pinhole. On the other side of the hole hold a paper screen.

You must do this in a completely darkened room. Then you will see a pale image of the candle appearing upside-down on the screen.

Experiment by altering the distance of the candle or paper screen from the pinhole, by enlarging the hole, or by pricking extra holes. Think about the changes you observe in the image.

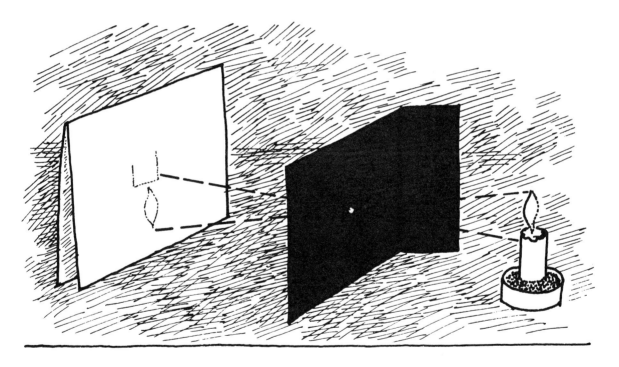

Light rays travelling straight from the bottom of the candle (object) must pass through the pinhole, and so they reach the upper part of the screen. Rays from the top of the candle reach the lower part of the screen. Rays in between act in similar ways. The result is an upside-down image that is dim, bright sharp or fuzzy – depending on the size of the hole and how far the light is allowed to spread before forming an image.

Our word "camera" comes from a Greek word meaning a cave-like room. Being inside your magic room is what it must be like inside a camera.

The wave theory of light

Waves of energy

When you pick up and throw a stone, you give it some energy or "go". If the stone drops into a pond, most of the energy is used to make the splash and to produce wave-like ripples – that seem to spread in ever-widening circles. Observing these ripples helps you to understand light waves and what we have been calling "rays".

The impact of the stone makes the water heave up and down. Water is made of particles called molecules that cling to each other, but are too small to see. Molecules at the center of the splash pass on their up-and-down motion to molecules next to them. These molecules also bob up and down and pass on their motion to other molecules. In this way, energy travels away from the center of the splash.

Only the energy travels. The water simply moves up and down as the little waves pass. (A cork floating on the pond just bobs up and down – it is not forced to go to the edge of the pond.)

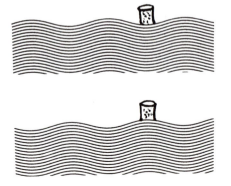

Tops and bottoms of water waves are called crests and troughs. The distance between one wave crest and the next is the "wave-length" and the number of wavelets passing the cork each second is the "frequency". Light waves are in several ways like this, but they travel in all directions (not just outwards).

Rays

A "ray" is a straight line drawn to show in a simple way how part of a system of light waves spreads out from the sun or a lamp to your eyes.

In your experiment with the sun and comb (page 10) you got visible "rays" by blocking some of the spreading light waves by the teeth.

Light consists of waves

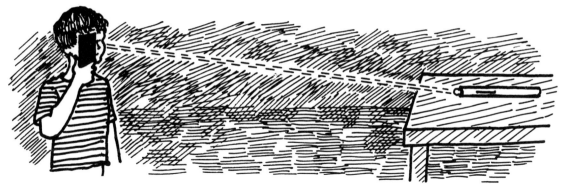

With a pin, prick two *tiny* holes *as close as possible to each other* in a piece of black paper. At the other end of a darkened room, put a lit flashlight (one of the "handy" small ones, without any glass over its bare bulb). Hold the pinholes close to one eye and look through them at the light.

You see a short line of thin, light bars, separated by thin, dark bars. This experiment might seem trivial, but it is one of the most important ones ever done in science. It proved that light must consist of waves.

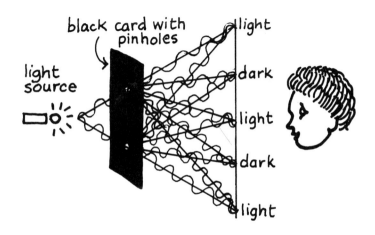

Explanation

When two water waves of equal force and wavelength overlap, two things can happen:

If their crests and troughs overlap exactly, they combine their strengths to make a higher crest and a lower trough. Where the overlap occurs the wave energy is stronger.

If the crest of one wave overlaps the trough of the other wave, their up-and-down motions cancel out. Where this happens there seems to be no energy.

The idea explains the light bars you see (where light wave crests and troughs overlap exactly) and the dark bars (where crests and troughs cancel out).

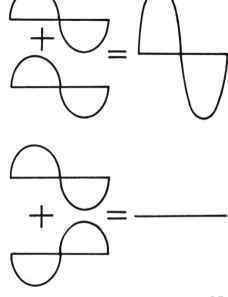

Seeing the rainbow

Sunlight reflected from a sheet of paper looks white, but if the light is allowed to pass through a prism, it spreads out to form a band of brilliant rainbow colors. If these colored lights are "caught" by a second prism, they can be put together again to make the original white. White is really a mixture of colors.

White light contains many different wave-lengths, from short-waved blues to long-waved reds. A prism can separate them by refracting each wave-length through a different angle. There are hundreds of wave-lengths, but the ones that our eyes and brain are constructed to recognize are those that can be seen in a rainbow.

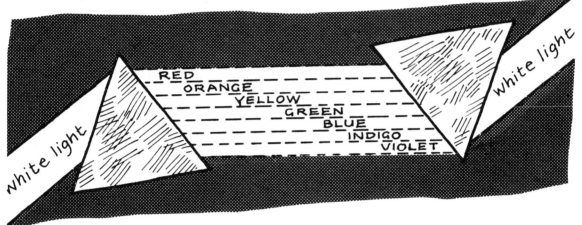

Color sense

When you focus an eye, light is made to fall on a particularly sensitive part inside the eye called the fovea. Here there are three sorts of color-sensitive cells called cones. Each kind reacts to a different collection of wave-lengths that you see as either red, blue or green – these are called the scientist's primaries (not to be confused with the artist's primaries).

Color sense depends on how you see proportions of primary red, blue and green waves. Red with green gives a sensation of yellow. Red with blue gives magenta. Blue with green gives an impression of cyan, or turquoise. These mixtures are called secondary colors. A pair of colors made up of a secondary plus the third primary (yellow/blue, magenta/green, cyan/red) are called complementary colors.

Some of the light hitting an object is absorbed by substances called pigments, some is transmitted (as through a window) and the remainder is reflected. The color of the object depends on which wave-lengths of light it reflects, or (if it is transparent) allows to get through.

You see a red poppy with its green leaves because its petals reflect mainly red, while its leaves reflect a mixture of waves that you see as light green. A yellow buttercup reflects a mixture of red and green. A marigold flower may reflect more red than yellow, so it looks orange-colored.

Mixing pigments

If you mix cyan (blue-green) pigment paint with yellow (red-green), you get green, because both pigments reflect green. Different blue-green or red-green proportions produce different greens. In a similar way, mixing yellow with magenta pigments makes red. Add black and it absorbs amounts of all colors – making a darker shade. Add white and it absorbs very little red, green and blue – making a brighter hue.

Mixing lights

You can also make colors by adding together different-colored lights – as is done on theatre and television stage sets.

In a dark room shine two flashlights through sheets of colored cellophane, one red and the other green. Where the light patches overlap on a white paper, you will see a yellowish color.

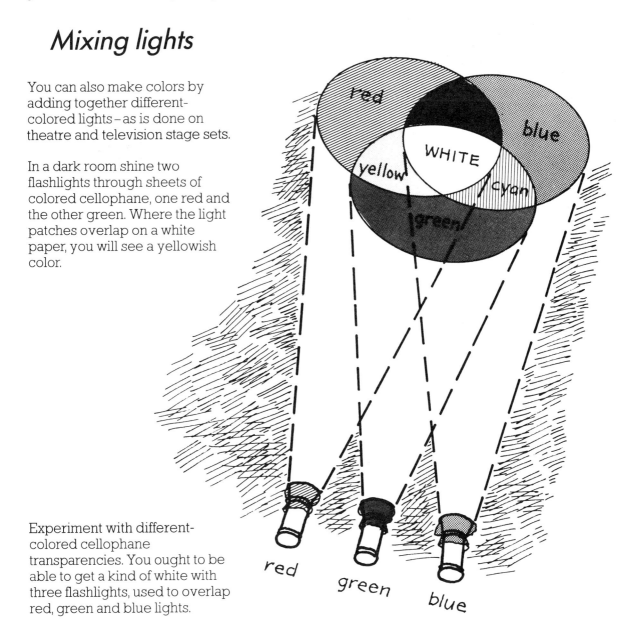

Experiment with different-colored cellophane transparencies. You ought to be able to get a kind of white with three flashlights, used to overlap red, green and blue lights.

More ghosts

Victorian parents bought "ghost books" to amuse their children on dark nights in winter. Make pages for your own ghost book by cutting out some shapes like these, using green, blue and yellow papers. Stick them on white papers. Stare at one of the "ghosts" for about 20 seconds, then look at a pale background in a corner of the room. There you see (or think you see) an after-image of the ghost in the complementary color of the original.

Remember that each of the three kinds of cone cells in the eye reacts to a different one of the primaries, red, green and blue. Light energy hitting a cone cell splits a pair of chemical substances inside the cell – to make a nerve signal to the brain. It takes a short while for the chemicals to join together again. Until that happens that particular cell loses its sensitivity.

green

If you stare at the green ghost you will tire your green cone cells, but give your red and blue cones a rest. After 20 seconds, when you stare at a pale wall or a sheet of white paper, you will not be very sensitive to green light coming from the wall or paper, so you see a ghost-shaped patch of combined red and blue light – a magenta-colored "ghost".

yellow

By now you should know enough color theory to be able to predict (tell before you try it) what colors the after-images will be, after you stare at the yellow and blue ghost pictures. Also notice how long your eyes take to recover and see normally again.

blue

Ghost puzzle

If you look for your ghost some distance away, it looks far bigger than the picture. Can you guess why this happens?

Colors from nowhere

Take a photostat copy of this black and white disc. Paste it on card, cut it out – and spin it clockwise on a pin. You see four rings of color, the outer one being blue. Spin the disc counter-clockwise and the order of the colors is reversed, the inner one appearing blue.

The "colors" also appear if the disc is spun while being televised in black and white. (Try this test if your school has closed-circuit TV.) Nobody can explain this illusion.

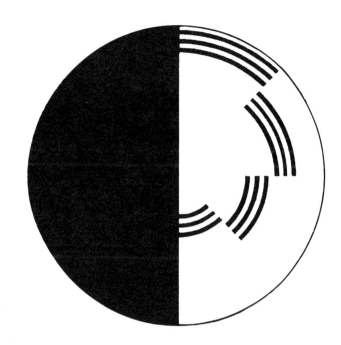

More puzzles

Predict what you might be able to see if you look at the spinning disc next to its image in a mirror.

(The image of the disc spinning clockwise will be a disc like this going counter-clockwise – a double reversal...)

Check your guess by doing a test.

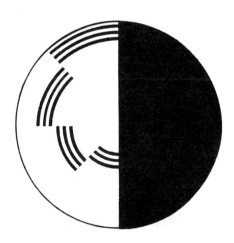

Also predict what you might be able to see if you look at the reflection of the spinning disc in a pair of mirrors, hinged together at 90° to each other.

Then do the test. This will make you think.

And, if you are still fascinated by colors that appear from nowhere, make up and test the other black and white disc pattern shown on the left.

Müller-Lyer's mystery

Spare a moment to be amazed by the magic of Müller-Lyer's famous "double arrows" optical illusion, invented a hundred years ago. The straight line between the arrowheads on the first figure (A) is the same length as the line between the inside-out arrows on figure (B). Yet you will (probably) have to admit that the line between the inverted arrows (B) looks longer.

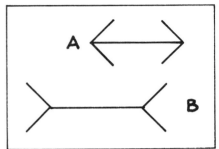

Perhaps your brain judges that line A is being squeezed and that line B is being stretched – an idea not unlike Müller-Lyer's own explanation.

Finding out how other people see the Müller-Lyer arrows

Draw the diagrams on a very large piece of cardboard (or use two pieces). In our own test we drew the main lines 18 in long and made the angles of the arrowheads 90°. You also need a black cardboard square and a ruler.

It is important that you always say and do the same things when getting people to take part in your experiment. Begin by admitting that it is an optical illusion, not a trick to catch them out.

Ask each person to cover line B with the card, so that A and B look equal in length. Then measure the uncovered part of the line to the nearest tenth of an inch. Put your findings on a graph.

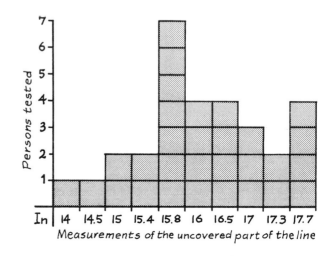

Measurements of the uncovered part of the line

Ideas for different experiments

The illusion is said to work best if the angles of the arrowheads are 60° and the sides of the "points" are a third of the length of the straight line between them. You could check out this idea.

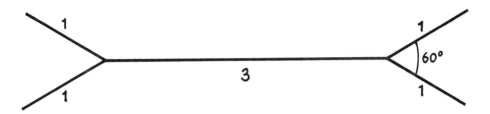

Younger people are said to see the illusion better than elderly people. You could test children, young adults and older persons (using the same number of people in each experiment) and compare graphs of your findings.

Müller-Lyer's illusion put to use in dress design . . .

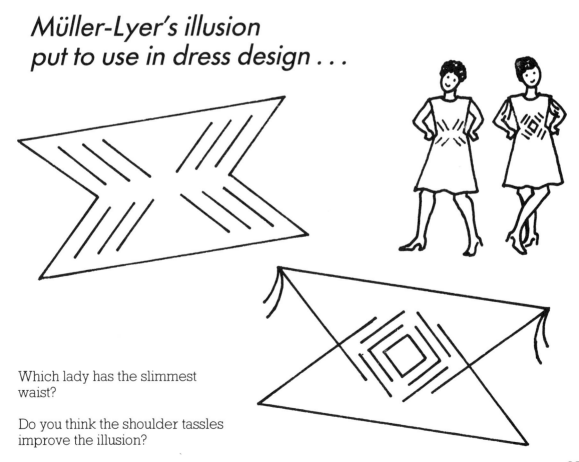

Which lady has the slimmest waist?

Do you think the shoulder tassles improve the illusion?

The baffling ball

Seeing takes a fraction of a second longer if the amount of light entering your eye is reduced. You might say that the eye takes longer to "develop" its pictures. Explore this idea with a dark lens from sunglasses and a golf ball, taped to a string and made to swing gently from side to side *in a straight line,* at eye-level, across your field of sight.

Watch the ball with both eyes wide open, while covering your left eye with the lens. To your amazement, the ball appears to be swinging in a circle.

Explanation

The dark lens stops a lot of light from going into your left eye, compared with the other eye. The result is that "seeing" with your left eye is a little late.

When the ball is still for an instant, at either end of its swing, this does not matter. It matters very much when the ball is moving fastest, in mid-swing.

Then your brain gets signals from your eyes, telling it that the ball is apparently in two places (1 and 2) at the same time. But you know that this is impossible. To make sense of this puzzle the brain "sees" the ball in the unreal third positions, 3a and 3b – where your eyes' lines of sight meet or cross.

When the ball is moving towards the right it looks further away (3a) and when moving left it looks closer (3b). At slower speeds its unreal position does not seem so extreme.

Your brain puts all this together and misinforms you that the ball is moving around in a circle.

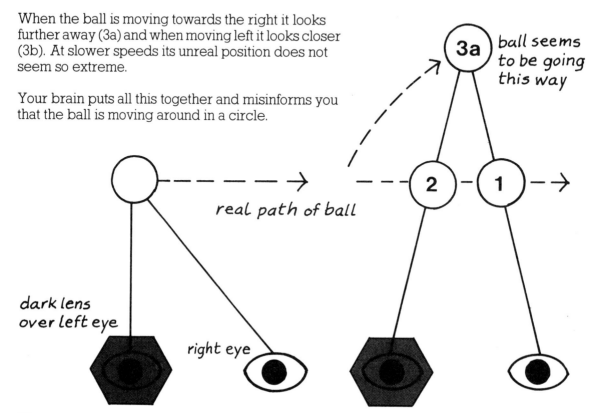

3a · ball seems to be going this way

real path of ball

2 · 1

dark lens over left eye

right eye

More experiments to try

1 Does the ball seem to go round the other way, when you watch it while holding the lens over the other eye?

2 Use this unusual way to look at things when you watch television. Do some of the TV pictures seem to have depth?

3 Another way to limit the amount of light entering an eye is to look through a hole between your fingers. Can you still see the optical illusion when you replace the lens with fingers?

Stereoscopic vision

You have stereoscopic vision (seeing in three dimensions, 3D, or "depth") because each eye gets a slightly different view of an object seen against a background.

Prove this by holding up your thumb at arm's length. Then notice how its position seems to change, when you look at it with one eye at a time.

The brain is sent two different pictures, but you do not "see double" because the brain combines the pictures – to give you a stereoscopic sense of distance. This is very useful when you are playing ball games or using tools, such as hammer and nails.

These ideas may help you to understand more fully the swinging ball mystery.

real path of ball

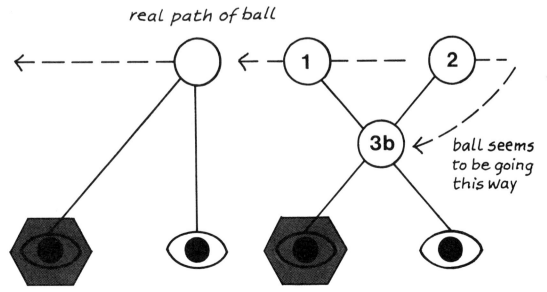

ball seems to be going this way

33

CIRCUS OF ILLUSIONS: Act 1

Seeing through a hole in your best friend's face

Hold a cardboard tube in your right hand. Close both eyes. Hold up the tube to your right eye. At the same time, hold up the palm of your left hand about 6 in in front of your (still shut) left eye.

Let the far end of the tube be pointing slightly over to the left. Then open both eyes at once – and wonder at the unbelievable vision you see of a hole through your hand. With a little imagination you should be able to work out a way to see a hole in the side of your friend's head.

This "magic" is done inside your head, when your brain combines two images.

Abracadabra – the lady vanishes

Paste a little cut-out picture of a girl from a magazine advertisement, about 6 in to the right of a white cross marked on a black card.

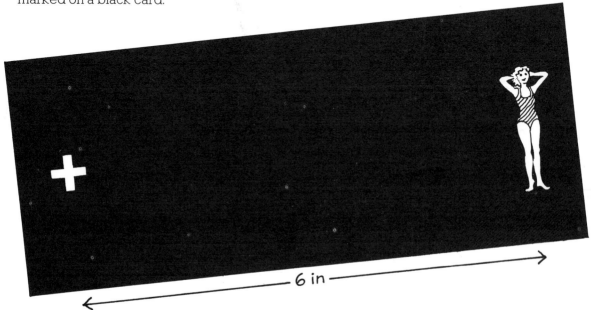

6 in

Close your left eye. Look with your right eye at the white cross. Hold the card at arm's length. Without actually focusing your eye on the girl, keep noticing her out of the corner of your eye. At the same time bring the card closer. *You must keep staring at the white cross.*

Suddenly the lady vanishes.

This happens because light reflected off the picture, coming into your eye, falls upon your eye's blind spot. This is the spot where bundles of nerves leave your eye, to make an optic nerve, and where there are no cells sensitive to light.

Find out if your left eye has a blind spot.

Flying saucery

Point your forefingers, tucking in the other fingers and thumbs, to make the hands look like pistols. Touch together the outstretched fingers – as if you were going to shoot the "guns" directly at each other. Hold them up (still touching) on a level with your eyes, at arm's length. While doing this, look at an object (a house across the street) while you notice the fingers without actually focusing your eyes on them. Then slowly draw the fingers apart.

There, between your fingers, you see a hovering "UFO".

It happens because, while you are focusing on the distant object, the images of nearby objects (your fingers), formed in your eyes, are too different for your brain to blend them together properly. You "see double" and the mental impressions of the fingertips overlap, to create the illusion of your "Flying Saucer".

CIRCUS OF ILLUSIONS: Act 2

Variations on a theme by Müller-Lyer

A

B

First variation
These are aircraft parked on an air field, seen from above. Which two pointed noses are further apart: A and B or B and C?

C

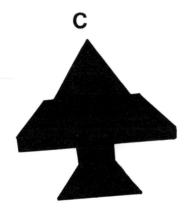

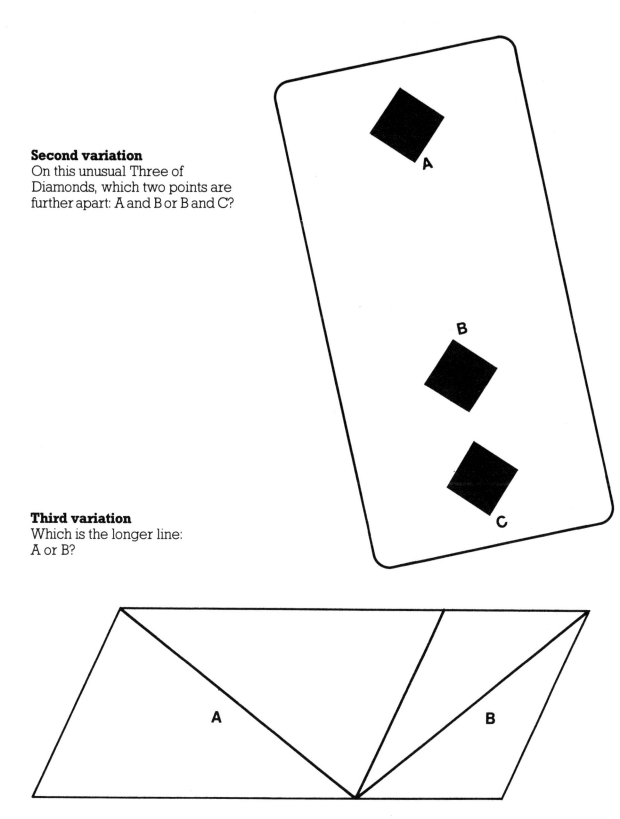

Second variation
On this unusual Three of Diamonds, which two points are further apart: A and B or B and C?

Third variation
Which is the longer line: A or B?

Measure all the distances. One of them is surprising.

CIRCUS OF ILLUSIONS: Act 3

Fake machinery

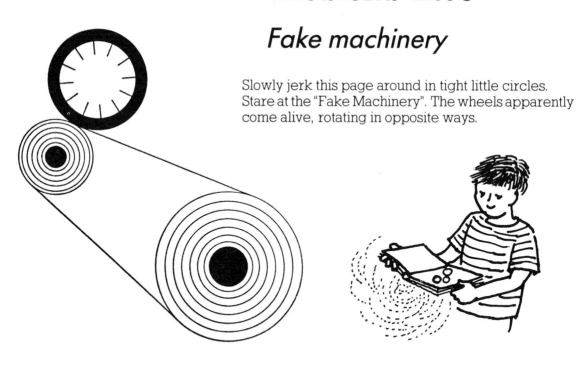

Slowly jerk this page around in tight little circles. Stare at the "Fake Machinery". The wheels apparently come alive, rotating in opposite ways.

Magic rings

Copy the two lines on a small rectangular card. Spin this diagram on a pin. You see two concentric circles. Why? On each line there is a point that rotates around the pin more slowly than any other point. These parts of the lines are less blurred while the card spins, so you see some magic rings.

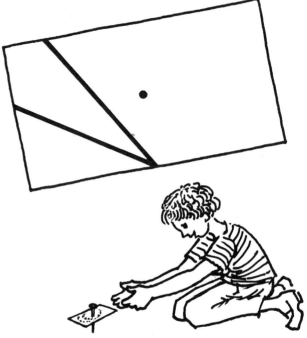

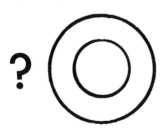

Coin ghost

Grip two coins, face to face, between your straightened first fingers. Slide the coins up and down by pressing them against each other. By "magic" that is all in the mind, you see a ghostly third coin appear between the others.

ghost

Clear pictures of each coin held still for an instant, between up-and-down movements, linger in eyes and brain. These impressions strengthen each other, and so you think you see the "coin ghost".

Disco

Copy the disc, paste it on card, cut it out and spin it slowly on a pin. Your brain interprets this unusual sight as a pair of black circles whirling around a white one – like a pair of hoola hoops being twirled round the waist of an agile body.

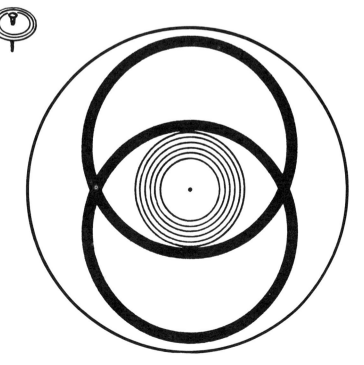

Judging distances

At short range

You have three-dimensional (3D) or stereoscopic eyesight at short range, because your two eyes look at an object from slightly different points of view. As you know, the brain puts together these slightly different views of the object, to form a single picture in depth.

This ability of eyes and brain helps you to judge how far things are away from you, at close range. Try threading a darning needle while using one eye only. It is much easier to do it with both eyes open.

At long range

In a town you observe how the buildings lining a street seem to get progressively smaller as you look into the distance, and so you decide that the street must be a long one. An artist or an architect calls these observations "perspective". In town and country, mists and haze seem to get denser with distance, blurring objects in the landscape. And you have also learned to understand slight changes in the pulls of muscles that focus your eyes, as clues to help you judge the distances of things at which you are looking.

Comparisons and feelings enable you to be fairly sure of your "sense of distance" on the ground, but they do not help much if you are looking up at airplanes, the sun or the moon. (**Of course, you never look directly up at the sun.**) With an airplane you need to see the head of the pilot, or to have recognized the type of airplane at an airport. There is, however, a special difficulty with the sun and moon. The sun is 93 million miles and the moon is 240 thousand miles away. Both distances are far beyond our earth-bound experience and imagination.

Variations in the vast distances from us of these huge objects in outer space do not change the size they are in the sky. This fact is not obvious. Their sizes must be measured.

The sun and moon illusion

At sunrise and sunset, when the sun is on the skyline, it looks much bigger than when it is above you at noon. The rising "harvest moon" that you notice on a summer's night looks gigantic, yet it appears much smaller when you see it overhead some hours later. These are remarkable optical illusions.

Your brain is baffled because it judges these sizes by comparisons with objects and perspective on the earth. The sun or moon on the horizon is compared with little hills and woods, so it looks relatively big. But compared with nearby treetops or buildings, the sun or moon looks relatively small. You can easily prove that the size does not change. But **only do this test by looking at the moon.** Remember that staring at the sun can make you go blind.

With the moon looking big on the horizon, hold some matches at arm's length. How many, side by side, are needed to cover the moon? Wait, and do the test again while the moon is looking smaller, above you. You will find that the same number of matches is needed.

Tricks of perspective

Here is a drawing in which perspective is exaggerated and three figures are drawn the same size. Compare the nearest man with the one in the distance. Which looks taller?

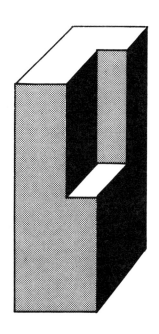

Is there a piece cut out from the large block, or a bit stuck on the corner? Then turn the drawing sideways. Now do you see a cut-away room with a raised platform?

Persistence of vision

You "see" a spot of light for about one tenth of a second after it has stopped shining in the world outside your eyes and brain. Vision "carries on" or persists – a process called "persistence of vision" by scientists.

If you swing around a sparkler, you produce what friends see as a big circle of starry fire. They see this illusion by their persistence of vision – the principle that explains how you see cinema pictures, television and video.

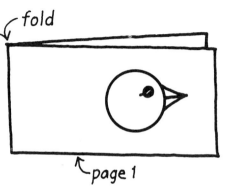

fold

page 1

Beak-snapping bird: the movie

Take a 2 x 10 in paper strip and fold it in two, to make a booklet. Draw a bird's head with a closed beak on page 1. But press hard with your pencil, to leave an impression on page 3. Then draw the same bird's head on page 3, but let the beak be open.

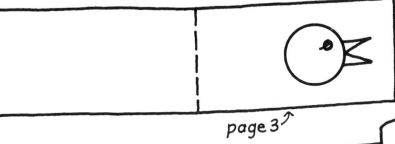

page 3

Roll page 1 tightly on to your pencil. It is important to be using good quality notepaper because the rolling is intended to put springiness into the paper. Now you will find that, by holding the "hinge" of the booklet with one hand, while you sweep the pencil to and fro sideways, the pictures appear in rapid succession – and you see a snapping bird.

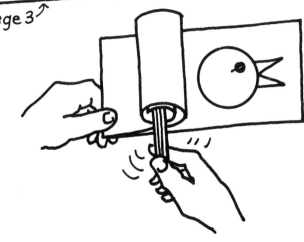

Each picture lingers in your mind for a fraction of a second, long enough for both pictures to blend – but in a wonderful way. Your brain "fills in" the gradual stages between the two pictures, and you sense motion.

On a reel of film (or coded electronically in videotape) there are tens of thousands of such pictures, each very slightly different, and your brain interprets the film or television pictures as a fair representation of life.

Other movies to make

A Hula-Hula dancer swinging her hips.

A boxer punching his opponent repeatedly.

A little old lady who keeps raising her hat.

A rude face that keeps poking its tongue out.

A clown bouncing up and down on a trampoline.

Keep all your subjects simple. Experiment with color. All the actions must be of the "one-two one-two" kind.

Magic – before your very eyes

Fix a piece of a *plastic* drinking straw on a safety pin. Strike a sharp blow on the plastic where shown in the picture. With practice, something magical happens. The straw seems to pass right through the steel pin. In actual fact it rebounds and flips around to the other side of the pin, but – with persistence of vision operating – you see the optical illusion.

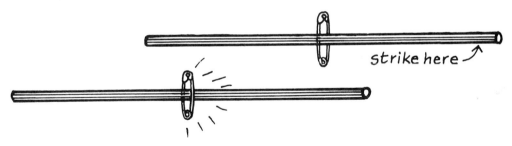

strike here

The first movies

150 years ago wealthier children were lucky enough to see the world's first movies. The pictures were drawn on discs called phenakistascopes, or on paper strips for viewing in a machine called a zoetrope.

Successive pictures in a sequence showed slight developments in a repetitive activity such as skipping, dancing, jumping up and down, or riding a circus horse. To prevent blurring, the pictures had to be seen one after the other, with a rest between each sighting. This was done by looking at the pictures through a series of slots. Black material between the slots acted like automatic shutters.

Movie projectors still have shutters, and there is a quick interval of darkness between each of the 30 separate pictures per second appearing on a TV screen.

Make photostat copies of the illustrations to make your own "Victorian" movies.

The phenakistascope

Paste the disc on cardboard. Cut it out, with its slots. Spin it on a nail, while you look through the slots at its reflection in a mirror.

The zoetrope

Paste the slotted strip on cardboard. Cut it out, then paste together its ends to form a cylinder having eight slots. (The end slots must overlap.)

Stand the cylinder on the turntable of a record-player – and let it turn at 33⅓ r.p.m. Look in through the slots to see the child skipping.

turntable

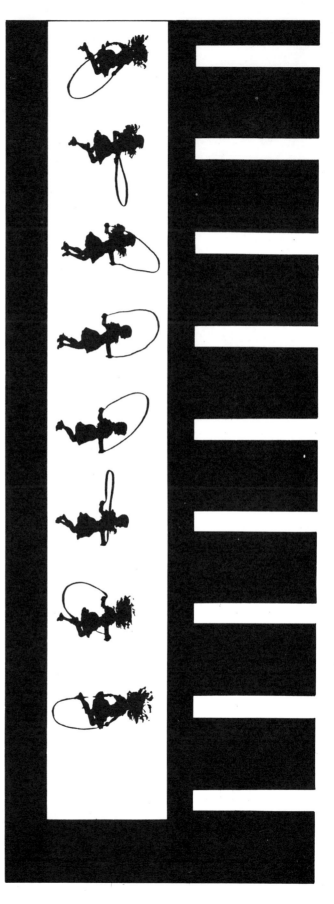

Television magic

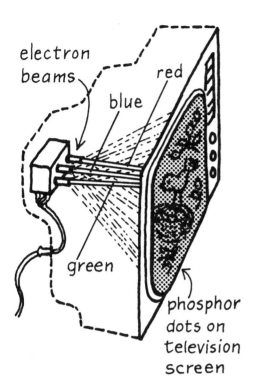

electron beams

red

blue

green

phosphor dots on television screen

Inside the picture tube of your color television set are three electronic "guns", aimed by magnets that fire three separate beams of electrons at the screen.

Each beam is a code of brightness or darkness for one of the three primary colors: red, green and blue. All the beams scan, or sweep across, the screen ten thousand times a second, to make pictures.

The beams are aimed to hit sets of three chemical spots called phosphors, each of which glows either red, green or blue when hit by its proper beam. There are many thousands of these phosphor sets. You can see them as round or rectangular colored dots on the screen. A special mask stops phosphors from being hit by the wrong beams.

Every second 25 complete pictures appear on the screen, each one made from lines of the colored dots. Between pictures, the screen goes dark. Your brain puts together this incredible amount of information – and you see a moving picture.

Magic from thin air

Put a slide of a funny face in a slide projector. Focus the projector to throw a clear image for a distance of six feet. Set up the projector to shine into the garden at night. Six feet away from the projector, wag a stick that is painted white. As the stick scans the beam from the projector, you "magic" a picture (made from strips of light) out of thin air.

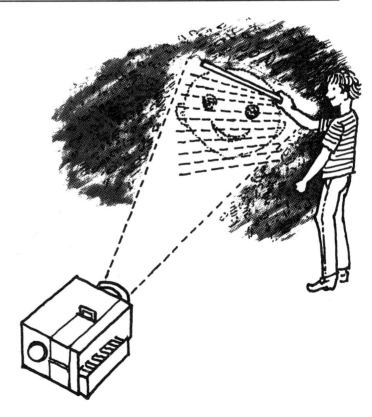

Caged bird

Fix a little card in a slot cut in a stick. On one side of the card draw a bird. Draw a cage on the other side. Roll the stick between your hands. The pictures appear in succession. A picture persists or lasts in your brain for about a tenth of a second. Your brain puts the pictures together to make one.

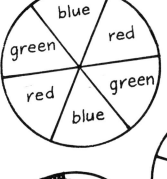

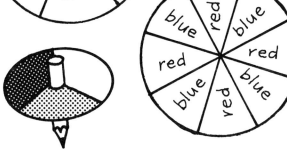

Mixing primaries to make other colors

Make little tops from cardboard circles and pencil stubs. Decorate the tops with sectors in various mixtures of the three primary colors (you can use paints or gummed papers). Spin the tops and watch different colors appear.

Flicker "stick"

Wag a pencil in front of a television picture. The screen lights up to make a fresh picture 25 times a second – producing many separate outlines of the moving pencil.

Index